California Megastorm:

Why Experts Warn of an Impending Megaflood in the Golden State

By Mark Reeves

Table of Contents

Chapter 1: What is an Outburst Flood / Megaflood?

A megaflood is a flood that quickly discharges a massive volume of water. In geomorphology, it is also termed an outburst flood. After the last ice age, several huge floods were triggered by the collapse of ice sheets or glaciers which built the dams of glacial lakes.

Examples of previous outburst floods are known from the geological history of the Earth. Landslides, lahars, and volcanic dams may block rivers and produce lakes. When the rock or earth barrier falls or is degraded, this generates a flood. Lakes also occur behind glacial moraines, which may collapse and cause outburst floods.

Oceans encompass 70% of the Earth's surface. And when tsunamis and megatsunamis are unleashed inside them, they create a danger and a risk to human life. But natural water-related risks aren't merely restricted to our seas. Floods are another danger, and like tsunamis and megatsunamis, there are numerous kinds of floods generated by diverse sources. Normal floods occur due to rainfall. When it rains softly, water may be absorbed into the earth. It then finds its way to rivers and flows away. But when it rains more severely, the sheer volume of water overwhelms the capacity of the earth to absorb it up and the ability of rivers to take it away.

The river then rises out of its banks and may invade cities and other inhabited places, causing damage, disruption, and risk to life. Specific situations, such as slow-moving rain clouds, severe rainfall, monsoons, or certain patterns of wind, may make flooding worse. But there's a limit to the amount of flooding that can happen since there's only so much rain that can fall over a particular length of time. This helps to limit the quantity of flooding that may be encountered. There is, however, a distinct form of flood, a more severe variety, termed a megaflood. It's different because instead of being produced by rainfall, megafloods are triggered by massive amounts of water being discharged from behind some type of storage.

Usually, this is a lake trapped behind a dam of some type, but it may also be water released from a glacier when a volcano erupts below it or when the sea rushes into a region that used to be dry ground. Sometimes we call this form of megaflood an outburst flood since it's triggered by water bursting out from one of these stores. Unlike floods, they don't merely depend on the quantity of rain that's fallen before and during the occurrence. They unleash water that's been built up over extended periods from many separate storms, and that means that megafloods have the potential to be considerably more catastrophic than floods.

But what sort of dams may cause a megaflood if they fail?

Well, the manmade dams that engineers create on rivers may undoubtedly cause megafloods if they collapse. The Banqiao Dam in China in 1975 and the Bento Rodrigues Dam accident in Brazil in 2015 both produced minor megafloods. But some of the most gigantic megafloods are created when huge natural dams constructed on rivers break. Natural dams may be constructed when a huge landslide or a glacier blocks a river. And the greater the landslide or glacier, the more water that's trapped and eventually discharged from behind it. Very slow increases in sea level may also generate megafloods from what were formerly oceans flooding enormous regions of previously dry land. Both of these circumstances may cause very enormous megafloods.

This sort of megaflood happened many hundreds of thousands of years ago in the Dover Straits between modern-day England and France. Previously, this location was a dry river valley, but the rising of surrounding sea levels led to as much as 1 million cubic meters of water per second flowing into the Dover Straits from the North Sea. That's enough water to fill 400 Olympic-sized swimming pools each second. This tremendous catastrophe converted what was once a broad, calm river valley into the deep, wide depression that fell by the sea that we see dividing England and France today. This is only one example of a megaflood that occurred long ago.

Megafloods are created by something altogether different than typical floods. Regular floods are generated by rainfall but megafloods are caused by a big amount of water being released from behind some form of storage.

Types of stores

-Artificial dams
Two severe incidents in our recent past we cited were both triggered by the breakdown of man made dams.

1975 Banqiao dam disaster, China
The breakdown of the dam resulted in 701 million cubic meters of water being spilled in 6 hours.

2015, Bento Rodriguez dam disaster, Brazil
Around 60 million cubic meters of iron waste was dumped into the Doce river and subsequently into the Atlantic ocean.

-Natural dams
Megafloods may also be produced by the breakdown of natural dams.

These are generated when a landslide or glacier blocks a river. If they are extremely huge they may hold massive volumes of water.

One recent example of a landslide obstructing a river occurred in Attabad, Pakistan. In 2010 a large landslide blocked the Hunza river and produced Attabad Lake.

Changes in sea level

Another source of megafloods is changes in sea level. This sort of megaflood transpired roughly 450,000 years ago in the Dover Straits, between modern-day England and France.

In this scenario, the Dover Straits which were originally a dry river valley was totally inundated owing to slow increases in sea level. This divided modern-day England and France.

This was a genuinely severe occurrence that had a lasting influence on our world.

Other instances of outburst floods throughout history include:

-The Black Sea (~7,600 years ago)

It is reported that a rising sea flood led to the replenishment of the freshwater glacial Black Sea with water from the Aegean. It is defined as "a rapid surge of salt water into a depressed fresh-water lake in a single tragedy that has been the foundation for the flood mythology".

The maritime intrusion was triggered by the increasing level of the Mediterranean around 7,600 years ago. It is the topic of discussion among geologists. The occurrence of the flood is not definite, and the hypothesis that it formed the foundation for subsequent flood stories is not established.

-The Caspian and Black Seas (about 16,000 years ago) (around 16,000 years ago)

A proposal suggested by Andrey Tchepalyga of the Russian Academy of Sciences dates the flooding of the Black Sea basin to an earlier period and from a different source. According to Tchepalyga, global warming starting around 16,000 years ago triggered the melting of the Scandinavian ice sheet. This created a tremendous river discharge which went into the Caspian Sea. The Caspian basin could not retain all the floodwater, which poured into the historic Black Sea basin. This would have inundated enormous regions that were formerly populated or utilized for hunting. Tchepalyga says this may have provided the foundation for traditions of the great Deluge.

-Refilling the Mediterranean (5.3 million years ago) (5.3 million years ago)

A devastating flood replenished the Mediterranean Sea 5.3 million years ago. The flood happened when Atlantic waves made their way through the Strait of Gibraltar into the Mediterranean basin, which was then a salt lake and salt bed.

-Glacial lake floods in North America

In North America at the glacial maximum, there were no Great Lakes as we know them. but "proglacial" (ice-frontage) lakes were created and moved. The most notable of these proglacial lakes was Lake Agassiz. Melting ice created a succession of huge floods from Lake Agassiz. Massive volumes of freshwater were added to the world's seas.

The last of the North American proglacial lakes, north of the existing Great Lakes, attained its greatest capacity approximately 8,500 years ago when combined with Lake Agassiz. But its exit was blocked by the vast wall of the glaciers and it flowed through tributaries into the Ottawa and St. Lawrence Rivers far to the south. About 8,300 to 7,700 years ago, the ice dam fell catastrophically. Lake Ojibway's beach terraces reveal that it was 250 meters (820 ft) above sea level. The capacity of Lake Ojibway is believed to have been roughly 163,000 cubic kilometers, more than enough water to cover a flattened-out Antarctica with a sheet of water 10 meters (33 ft) deep. That amount was added to the world's seas in a couple of months.

The specific timing and rates of change following the commencement of melting of the big ice sheets are issues of continuous investigation.

Chapter 2: The Great Flood of 1862

The Great Flood of 1862 was the biggest in the documented history of Oregon, Nevada, and California, happening from December 1861 to January 1862. It was preceded by weeks of heavy rains and snows at the extremely high altitudes that started in Oregon in November 1861 and persisted into January 1862. This was followed by a record amount of rain from January 9–12, and contributed to a flood that extended from the Columbia River southward in western Oregon, through California to San Diego, and extended as far inland as Idaho in the Washington Territory, Nevada, and Utah in the Utah Territory, and Arizona in the western New Mexico Territory.

The event poured approximately equivalent to 10 feet (3.0 m) of water across California, in the form of rain and snow, over a period of 43 days. Immense snowfalls in the mountains of far western North America triggered further floods in Idaho, Arizona, and New Mexico, as well as in Baja California and Sonora, Mexico the following spring and summer, when the snow melted.

The event was topped with a warm vigorous storm that melted the heavy snow burden. The subsequent snow-melt swamped valleys, inundated or washed away cities, mills, dams, flumes, homes, fences, and domestic animals, and destroyed fields. It has been characterized as the greatest tragedy ever to hit California. The storms caused roughly $100 million 1861 USD in damage, approximately equivalent to $3.117 billion (2021 USD) (2021 USD). The governor, state legislature, and state workers were not paid for a year and a half. At least 4,000 people were reported to have been killed in the floods in California, which was nearly 1% of the state population at the time.

Impact on California

California was slammed by a mix of relentless rain, snow, and then abnormally hot temperatures. In Northern California, it snowed extensively throughout the second half of November and the first few days of December, when the temperature reached exceptionally high until it started to pour. There were four different rainy periods: The first occurred on December 9, 1861, the second on December 23–28, the third on January 9–12, and the fourth on January 15–17.

Native Americans recognized that the Sacramento Valley might become an inland sea when the rains arrived. Their storytellers recounted water overflowing the valley from the Coast Range to the Sierra.

-Northern California

Fort Ter-Waw, situated in Klamath Glen, California, was damaged by the flood in December 1861 and abandoned on June 10, 1862. Bridges were swept away in Trinity and Shasta counties. At Red Dog in Nevada County, William Begole stated that from December 23 to January 22 it poured a total of 25.5 inches (650 mm), and on January 10 and 11 alone, it rained almost 11 inches (280 mm) (280 mm).

At Weaverville, John Carr was a witness to the fast melt of snow by the heavy rain and commencement of the flood in December 1861 on the Trinity River:

From November through the later half of March there was a sequence of storms and floods... The land was blanketed with snow 1 foot [30 cm] thick, and on the mountains even deeper... The water in the river ... appeared like some gigantic uncontrolled monster of devastation ripped loose from its chains, pouring wildly forward, and everywhere spreading ruin and disaster along its route. When rising, the river appeared highest in the middle... From the head settlement to the mouth of the Trinity River, over a distance of one hundred and fifty miles, everything was washed to ruin. Not a bridge was left, or a mining wheel or a sluice-box. Parts of ranches and miners' cottages suffered the same fate. The efforts of hundreds of men, and their savings of years, spent in bridges, mines, and ranches, were all washed away. In forty-eight hours the valley of the Trinity was left barren. The county never recovered from the terrible disaster. Many of the mining wheels and bridges were never restored.

Two years later William H. Brewer witnessed in Crescent City, the wreckage of the flood:

The floods of two years ago brought down a huge quantity of driftwood from all the rivers along the coast, and it was tossed up along this portion of the shore in amounts that defy belief. It appeared to me as though I saw enough in 10 miles down the beach to create a million cords of wood... One I measured was 210 feet [64 m] long and 3 1/2 feet [1.1 m] at the tiny end, without the bark.

-Central Valley

The whole Sacramento and San Joaquin valleys were swamped. An region roughly 300 miles (480 km) long, averaging 20 miles (32 km) in width,[21] and encompassing 5,000 to 6,000 square miles (13,000 to 16,000 km2) was under water.[15] The water flooding the Central Valley reached depths up to 30 feet (9.1 m), fully drowning telegraph poles that had recently been constructed between San Francisco and New York. Transportation, mail, and communications throughout the state were affected for a month. Water inundated areas of the valley from December 1861, through the spring, and into the summer of 1862.

The rainy season began on the 8th of November, and for four weeks, with barely any pause, the rain continued to fall quite softly in San Francisco, but in heavy showers in the interior. According to the assertion of a Grass Valley publication, nine inches of rain fell there in thirty-six hours on the 7th and 8th inst.... the following day the river-beds were full nearly to the hilltops. The North Fork of the American River at Auburn climbed thirty-five feet, and in many other mountain streams, the increase was nearly as significant. On the 9th the water reached the low ground of the Sacramento Valley.

In Knight's Ferry, in the foothills of the Sierra Nevada astride the Stanislaus River, about 40 miles (64 km) east of Modesto, the town's residences, its mill, and most of its businesses were damaged by the flood. The bridge crossing the river initially resisted the flood levels but was destroyed when the wreckage of the bridge at Two-Mile Bar, just a short distance up the river, ripped from its foundation, and smashed against the Knights Ferry Bridge, smashing the truss supports and knocking it off its rock base. All Sacramento, including one street, part of Marysville, part of Santa Rosa, part of Auburn, part of Sonora, part of Nevada City, and part of Napa were under water. Some smaller cities like Empire City and Mokelumne City were utterly devastated.

-Sacramento

Sacramento, sited at the confluence of the Sacramento and American Rivers, was initially constructed at 16 feet (4.9 m) above low-water level, and the river generally rose 17 to 18 feet (5.2 to 5.5 m) virtually every year. The New York Times stated on January 21, 1862, that a trapper who had spent more than 20 years in California had repeatedly boated over the city's site, and in 1846, the water at the spot was 7 feet (2.1 m) deep for sixty days. [24] On 27 December 1861, the Sacramento River reached a flood level of 22 feet 7 inches (6.88 m) over the low water mark, after rising 10 feet (3.0 m) within the prior 24 hours.

The Sacramento flood plain swiftly became occupied by a rising population during the Gold Rush and functioned as the principal center for business and trade and the site of political authority, the California State Legislature. The landscape was recognized as a flood-prone landscape located at the confluence of the American and Sacramento Rivers. John Muir highlighted the intensity of yearly flooding in Sacramento, "...The largest floods come in winter, when one may assume all the wild streams would be muffled and imprisoned in frost and snow... rare intervals of warm rains and warm winds invade the mountains and push back the snow line from 2000 to 8,000 feet, or even higher, and then come to the big floods."

However, the series of storms that led to the Great Flood of 1862 averaged precipitation levels that records show only occur once every 500 to 1,000 years. The geographical range of floods in the state was documented by a traveling geologist from Yale University, William Brewer, who stated that on January 19, 1862,

The enormous Central Valley of the state is under water—the Sacramento and San Joaquin valleys—a territory 250 to 300 miles long and an average of at least 20 miles broad, a district of 5,000 or 6,000 square miles, or maybe three to three and a half million acres! Although most of it is not farmed, nevertheless a section of it is the garden of the state. Thousands of farms are fully underwater—cattle suffering and dying.

From December to January 1862 the succession of storms delivering strong winds and heavy rains left city streets and walkways submerged. Photographs depict canals in place of city streets and boats anchored to stores.

On Inaugural Day, January 10, 1862, the state's ninth governor, Leland Stanford, went by rowboat to his inauguration building held at the State Legislature office. Much of Sacramento remained underwater for 3 months after the storms passed. As a consequence of the floods, the California State Legislature was temporarily transferred to San Francisco for rebuilding and reconstructing the drowned city of Sacramento.

Levee damage

The city of Sacramento sustained the heaviest damage owing to its levee, which is situated in a broad and flat valley at the intersection of the American and Sacramento rivers. When the floods came from the higher terrain on the east, the levee worked as a barrier to retain the water in the city rather than allow it to flow out. Soon the water level was 10 feet (3.0 m) higher within than the level of the Sacramento River on the outside.

John Carr writes of his riverboat ride up the Sacramento River while it was at one of its peak phases of the flood:

... I was a passenger aboard the old steamship Gem, from Sacramento to Red Bluff. The only way the pilot could identify where the course of the river was, was by the cottonwood trees on either side of the river. The boat had to stop several times and take men out of the tops of trees and off the roofs of houses. On our drive up the river, we observed property of every sort flowing down—dead horses and cattle, lambs, pigs, homes, haystacks, family furniture, and everything conceivable was on its way to the ocean. Arriving in Red Bluff, there was water everywhere as far as the eye could reach, and what little bridges there had been in the land were all washed away.

Dozens of wood houses, some two stories high, were simply lifted and carried off by the flood, as was "all the firewood, most of the fences and sheds, all the poultry, cats, rats and many of the cows and horses". The Chinese in their poorly constructed shantytowns were disproportionately impacted.

A chain gang was despatched to rip down the levee, which, when it eventually collapsed, enabled the floods to surge out of the city center and dropped the level of the inundation by 5–6 feet (1.5–1.8 m) (1.5–1.8 m). Eventually, the floods receded to a level on par with the lowest portion of the city. From January 23, 1862, the state capital was transferred from flooded Sacramento to San Francisco.

City rebuilding

Politicians addressed the flood danger with an expenditure of more than $1.5 million on flood control and prevention via an enhanced levee system surrounding Sacramento and the larger Sacramento area.

Sacramento put efforts into restructuring the city's foundation by re-channeling the American River, reinforcing the established levee system, and passing a two-decade project to raise the city above flood level. Due to the high costs associated with flood recovery, the city of Sacramento reached out to the aid of the Transcontinental Railroad Co., which was a major turning point in levee resilience and reconstruction. Before the great flood, levee breaks and failures caused much destruction from flooding. The Transcontinental Railroad had laid tracks across the Sierra Nevada and stationed its major repair and production line in Sacramento. The Chinese crew of approximately 14,000 restored levees under the leadership of Charles Crocker, the chief contractor for Central Pacific Railroad.

In response to a poor levee system and periodic floods, flood plain architecture was included in residential infrastructure, visible in Victorian structures spanning Midtown to Downtown Sacramento. Flood design incorporates high front porches with steps running down to the street. In addition, tiny hollow chambers are placed into the basement level to allow for basement flooding and aeration.

Old Town Sacramento was elevated 15 feet above flood level. Ruins of the old city remain underneath the streets as tunnels leading nowhere, with hollow sidewalks, filled with entrances, trap doors, and rubble where storefronts and walkways used to be.

Large wooden beams and earth brought in from neighboring regions helped to stabilize and establish a foundation on top of the once-flooded city.

-Southern California

In Southern California, starting on December 24, 1861, it poured for 28 days in Los Angeles. In the San Gabriel Mountains, the mining town of Eldoradoville was washed away by flood waters. The storm destroyed hundreds of animals and wiped away fruit trees and vineyards that thrived along the Los Angeles River. No mail was received in Los Angeles for five weeks. The Los Angeles Star stated that:

The road from Tejon, we hear, has been practically swept away. The San Fernando mountain cannot be traversed save via the ancient path ... across the top of the mountain. The plan has been split up into gulches and arroyos, and streams are flowing down every declivity.

The lowlands of Los Angeles County, at the time a marshy region with numerous tiny lakes and multiple meandering streams from the mountains, were substantially inundated, and much of the agricultural production that lay along the rivers was damaged. In most of the lower areas, small settlements were submerged. These flooded areas formed into a large lake system with many small streams. A few more powerful currents cut channels across the plain and carried the runoff to the sea.

In Los Angeles County, (including what is now Orange County) the overflowing Santa Ana River caused an inland sea lasting approximately three weeks with water standing 4 feet (1.2 m) deep up to 4 miles (6 km) from the river. In February 1862, the Los Angeles, San Gabriel, and Santa Ana Rivers merged. Government assessments at the time suggested that a solid sheet of water covered the region from Signal Hill to Huntington Beach, a distance of roughly 18 miles (29 km) (29 km).

In Santa Barbara County, the limited coastal lowlands were flooded by the rivers coming out of the highlands. The San Buenaventura Mission Aqueduct that was still gathering water from a branch of the Ventura River for the town of Ventura water system was abandoned owing to the devastation in the region that became the independent Ventura County in 1873.

In San Bernardino County, all the lush riverbank fields and all but the church and one home of the New Mexican town of Agua Mansa, were carried away by the Santa Ana River, which overflowed its banks. A local priest rang the church bell on the night of January 22, 1862, warning the population of the approach of the flood, and everyone survived.

In San Diego, a storm at sea backed up the flood water rushing into the bay from the San Diego River, resulting in a new river channel carved into San Diego Harbor. The persistent heavy rain also transformed the aspect of the area, the formerly rounded hills were widely sliced by gullies and canyons.

To the north, in the Owens Valley, identical snow and flooding circumstances as those to the east in Aurora, Nevada (see below), led to the local Paiute suffering the loss of most of the game they relied on. Cattle, recently brought into the valley to feed the miners, competed with the natural grazers and ate the native wild plant harvests the Paiute relied on to live. Starving, the Paiute started to slaughter the cattle, and confrontation with the cattlemen ensued, culminating in the later Owens Valley Indian War.

Economic impact

In March 1862, the Wool Growers Association reported that 100,000 sheep and 500,000 lambs were killed by the floods. Even oyster beds in San Francisco Bay near Oakland were reported to be dying from the effects of the immense amounts of freshwater entering the bay. Full of silt, it buried the oyster beds. One-quarter of California's estimated 800,000 cattle were killed by the flood, hastening the downfall of the cattle-based ranchero community. One-fourth to one-third of the state's property was destroyed, and one house in eight was swept away or devastated by the floodwaters. Mining equipment such as sluices, flumes, wheels, and derricks was hauled away throughout the state.

An early estimate of property loss was $10 million. However, eventually, it was estimated that nearly one-quarter of the taxable real estate in the state of California was destroyed in the storm. The state nearly had to declare bankruptcy owing to the price of the destruction and the loss of tax income.

Chapter 3: How Climate Change Could Cause History to Repeat Itself in the Golden State

A recent research raises fears about climate change-fueled floods raining large volumes of water on drought-plagued California — an implausible seeming scenario that as said previously has occurred before.

While harsh droughts, wildfires, and earthquakes are often the major worries throughout the West, the report published recently warns of another problem approaching in California: "Megafloods." It warns climate change is increasing the danger of floods that might drown cities and displace millions of people throughout the state. It believes an exceptional monthlong storm may send feet of rain — in some spots, more than 100 inches – across hundreds of miles of California.

Though it happened 160 years ago, the flood – termed a "megastorm" for its record rainfall covering broad parts of the state – indicates that the danger is not only theoretical.

In reality, the UCLA experts investigating "megafloods" claim such storms normally happen every 100-200 years.

Researchers are ringing the alarm because floods of similar size now would have significantly more destructive consequences in a state that is now the nation's most populated.

And the Great Flood of 1862 was also preceded by drought. The researchers behind the study stated their results indicate that climate change "is significantly increasing both the frequency and amplitude of very severe storm sequences capable of triggering megaflood occurrences in California," making such an event more probable.

Climate change increases the quantity of rain the atmosphere can contain and causes more water in the air to fall as rain, which may lead to immediate floods. Both are and will continue to occur in California.
The new analysis demonstrates a fast rise in the chance of week-long, recurrent strong-to-extreme atmospheric rivers during the cold season.

An atmospheric river is a long, narrow zone of high moisture in the atmosphere that may deliver moisture hundreds of kilometers, like a fire hose in the sky. They normally offer helpful rains to drought-prone places like California but might swiftly turn harmful with a changing environment.

Historically these winter atmospheric rivers dump feet of snow in the Sierra Nevada, but as the climate warms, more of the snow will fall as rain. Instead of melting slowly over time, it all flows off, stacks up, and floods instantly.

With a neighbor like the Pacific Ocean, California has "a limitless reserve of water vapor offshore," experts noted.
California's steep geography and wildfire danger make it particularly susceptible to floods. Lingering burn scars from wildfires may provide a steep, slippery surface for water and debris to pour down. With wildfires increasing bigger and burning more land because of climate change, more regions are exposed to catastrophic debris flows.

Although models predict this megaflood is imminent, scientists argue there are methods to avoid excessive damage.

"I believe the magnitude of (megaflood) damages may be greatly decreased by doing certain types of things to redesign our flood control and our water management systems and our disaster preparation," says Daniel Swain, a climate scientist with UCLA and a researcher participating in the study.

Huang, a project scientist at the National Center for Atmospheric Research and a researcher participating in the study, said everyone may make a tiny contribution to mitigating climate change.
"If we work collectively to limit future emissions, we can also lessen the danger of severe occurrences," Huang added.